Melting Faces in a Cracked Mirror:

Written Works by E.D. Small

E.D. Small

Melting Faces in a Cracked Mirror:
Written works by E.D. Small

Book Cover Designer © Brittany Baum
Interior Illustrations © Natalie Duffy
Editing and Typesetting by Bianca Bowers

Printed and bound in the USA

Print ISBN-13: 978-1-7367323-0-4
epub ISBN-13: 978-1-7367323-1-1

Table of Contents

Word of mouth comes bittersweet.
So pick & choose ripe words to eat.

E.D. Small

black rose (from nothin')

watch as I give birth

to an embryo of hope

now watch my thoughts

as they steadily overt

feed them knowledge

watch them build strength

watch a black rose sky

from the soil of the hurt

melting faces in a cracked mirror
(if your hero were a zero)

if your hero were a zero,

would your dreams also shatter

before having time to matter?

staring at a raging globe,

young menacing peepholes.

snake-bit chiseled carbonado black diamond.

no photogenic flashy kodak moments.

if you are searching for my star, keep climbing!

beneath every freeway sprouts

a burgeoning forest, anew

where soulless remains of old nations rest.

why are natives made to resemble

the wild boar?

and the pilgrim,

the bean & lawn munching ewe?

(your wails don't fall on plugged ears)

on an election day, sunny-side-up,

saw a maga hat on a center city bus.

he stood and shouted, **"shapeshifters are amongst us!"**

atop reptilian scales they are finely clothed.

some with black, brown, or foreign pigmentation!"

this sudden mind-invasion serves as revelation,

why some hover a-round in space of alienation.

"hatred for one man is blinding a whole silly generation,"

a delegation of trumpeters is stating,

along with what some may consider an *obamac*nation,

"fake news is on every tv station!"

yet never strain a fiddle to that **"i can't breathe"** situation,

or those barkstiff brownskin fruits flailing like sausage trees.

flies blending with the wicked stale rotting breeze,

ghost faces with blood on their hands, **"blood on the leaves,"**

are we supposed to believe people noosed themselves intentionally?

you erase the *black*board of our american history,

"let's turn their ancient roots into an unsolved mystery,"

allowing us not to recognize the kings & queens we are?

if you want to find my favorite star…..

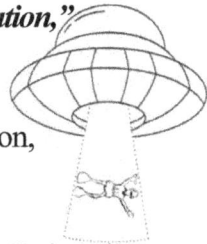

staring at a raging globe,

young menacing peepholes.

snake-bit chiseled carbonado black diamond.

no photogenic flashy kodak moments.

if you are searching for my star, keep climbing!

another no name in the streets

i saw great women, leaders of color

pinstripe warpaint

rise above horizons of crimson skies.

bridging poll lines of racial harmony,

aiding rescue of us,

no names in the streets

we are a barren field

with no flowers to be plucked,

without you.

no closed hollows to trap raindrops,

without your mighty leadership.

In the powerful vocals of Dr. Maya Angelou

I felt the fighter spirit of Sojourner Truth,

"Ain't I a woman?"

you are so much more

than this world will confess

In you we have found a

confident tongue

in a world where we are all

fighting for survival,

but no one wants to live,

together

It is time to unlatch

every birdcage,

Liberate the songbirds,

Resurrect our hope.

We stand and we fall,

but we rise every time

And we now know our names,

all because of you.

the american caterpillar

i am the american caterpillar

i am not your nigger, not your negro,

not your nigga

i am browning of red orchard fruit

minutes after first chomp

i am the insignificant seed

you spat on the sidewalk

i descended from tribal africans

who were stolen by foolish man

who were shipped across bloody sea

& auctioned on american land

who descended from warriors

then ascended from war

"in the land of the free"

where so many are poor

i am still the american caterpillar

hived in all colors, shapes & sizes

from honkytonk country landside

to slumdog ghetto high rises

i am the proud obnoxious dancer

i am the results of a broken home

streets where white-on-white &

black-on-black crime coincide

i boldly hold up my picket sign

reading "all police brutality

will now be televised!"

i am no longer an american caterpillar

now, i am a glitter-dusted african moth

travelling high for peace & liberty

'cause now i am with my wings

i am not white mass-murderer free

on schools & church killing sprees

nor am i freer than the entitled bigot

yelling, "go back to your country!"

but i am a soaring, talking riot

freedom fighting is not violent

no, i won't remain silent!

i am the american caterpillar

i am not your nigger, not your negro,

not your nigga

liberty is a waggish puddle in mid-desert

pretending to be a pillar of hope

mirage caused by john crow the drooling buzzard

but his pappy is jim crow

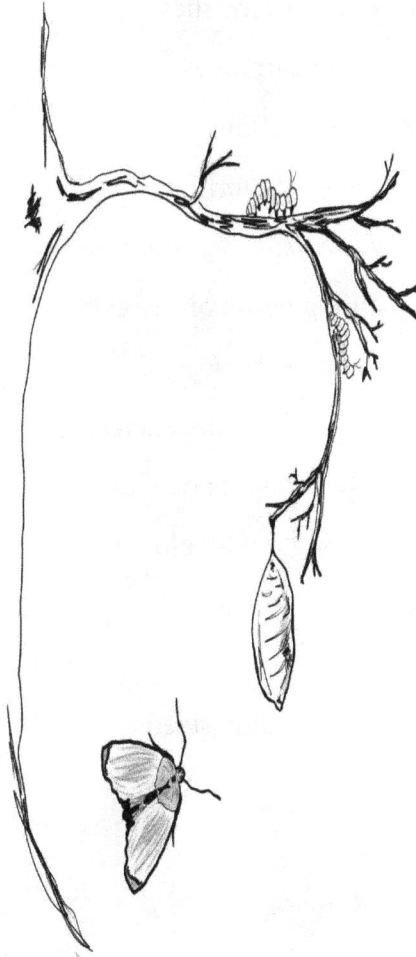

harriet tubman: the hummingbird & the wild horse

we are awakened by late brightness

could it be my beautiful gloomshine?

a golden figure who never tarnishes,

with delicate nature she harnesses

loose hairs of fading dandelions

silhouettes of rainbowed flutterflies,

all who dares to take to skies decorates disguise.

as i peep through sliding doors of my eyes,

I am directed by a sudden chime,

her bold movement leaves me mesmerized

as she gathers from sweet wild horse daylilies

then free wings commingle with clear fleeing breeze

long i have pleaded my sympathy

to simply *BE*

lifted from a chamber of stable steeds

is it kismet or of figment

for wild freed horses

to also fly in reign of victory?

creama wheat mornings
(a redacted false childhood)

at the break of each dawn

a crow would stridently screech,

all its bickering constantly irked.

this awakened an old hackneyed rooster,

who'd tardily go berserk.

every start of each morning

they'd make my ears hurt,

as they'd disquietly continue

to peeve like clockwork.

over yawning dew round table meetings,

which seated us.

poor is not what we realized we were.

pasty oats were disheartening days.

creama wheat sit-downs were early school release,

with a pitstop at the favorite burger shack.

i'd have a carrot nose if i said struggle had a repulsive taste.

our delicious flash bowl porridges were a sign of the times,

for us nubian goats in perpendicular wasteland.

dairy cream was cheap: sugar was cheaper.

if used, churned butter was cheap.

almost everything of little value is said to devalue us.

i wonder if the delusion on the box saw a fair pocket share?

that man who was used to magneto, the body-geared knights.

did he fred-rock the world's first phat motorcar?

dazing through futuristic sunglasses

at the back of a chauffeur's deciduous bean sprout.

was he ever recipient of a "happy vacation" bottle-carded message,

while sipping hula hula girl coconut drinks on an only rich folk island?

back home still having to pull his shutters down over his window vision,

in avoiding pass-through of every chauvinist toilet mouth.

why not another kitchen genius to harp on, for us?

why do others get to celebrate a caricature,

of us, for us? never with us.

yet another fictional made-to-be inarticulate

representation, apparently for us.

never have i seen a well-respected man

sleep in an *unmarked colored grave* for over 70 years

before the world realized he was a real person,

with a real name.

they say, "*as black america, you should be proud,*"

as if to say, be happy we are giving you "negroes" anything!

all i got to say about that is:

"*cash, rules, everything, around, me*

c.r.e.a.m.

get the money

dollar, dollar bill y'all."

hell no!!! we are not proud!!!

the path i should have followed
(after robert frost)

three paths intertwined,

in a green forest-pine

i found it hard to decide,

which path would be mine

the first path was *curved,*

so its ways were swerved

in no way, shape, or form

could it have ever been subserved

there were two wooden arrows,

pointing in different directions

one arrow *no name,*

the other arrow *keep stepping*

i travelled *keep stepping*

until my hairs turned grey

after years of wasting time,

i turned back the other way

it begged me to stay,

dirt & shrubs overlaid its road

the journey home was long –

by long i mean cold

it burrowed,

almost causing me to fall for its cajole

almost looped me like a chicken-

with those gangling catchpoles

the other path with *no name,*

was a little-known road at the time

it glossed and enticed.

exposing sets of quarried stone

i travelled this road for only one night

its remnants were so trite

constant coming & going during day

left me dashing-away in fright

please forgive me

for being particular

i am truly ashamed

path i should have followed

was *no name*

i now regret running off

once the daylight came

should have jostled

through the crowd

to stake my claim

there are longitudes to life

where paths may change

but i guess being *stone-blind*

deserves the blame

harlemniscent langston love story
(cinderella of peach tree circle)

green leaves, warm colors, autumn

decorating my public-housing building staircase,

remembrances of a stained-glass love emanate.

our momentary nighting was empty

to a drained colorless room,

we clinked glasses of a drink i don't remember

under sky of twinkling sand spurs

we merry-go-round to the atmosphere's movement,

your arms rested upon my shoulders,

silver painted nails interlocked hill of my back,

my palms surfed contours of your body waves.

two heart violins stroked to kindle fiery romance.

nightly cherry honeymoon horizons

i foresaw in your dazing crystal balls,

in them i saw the greatest romance story never told,

in them i longed to see proof of heaven.

"by any chance are you an angel?"

my amazing afrocentric au naturel queen to-hopefully-be.

your nature was a reggaeton wild night,

aura radiant enough to offset actions of any ballroom,

knitting my every movement,

like a helpless wood-boy marionette,

with such breath thieving goddess mystique.

powder-soft shea butter skin,

curly bush hair guarding a crouching temple of wisdom,

i cradled your insecurities like single parent bottle feeders,

from a bed of compost over dirt,

from baby stem to a-wakened stretching wildflower.

oh woman! i was in your garden.

you were mine for the taking,

before vanishing with hymn of day's end.

your red glitter bottom slipper,

i will sword and shield.

until tarot cards reveal me as your knight.

on days of storm,

cold nights of winter,

my life is mingled

out of kilter,

of all the moments

i remember,

is holding you in my arms,

until the day was gone,

until the day was gone.

(please come back to me my love)

blankest stares in history
(return of the buffalo soldier)

bolts of shock darters flash-land

on wasted soil of an unmarked boneyard,

while startled but wayworn weary-wolves,

tippy-claw further into the boondocks.

skeletor fists seesaw in-and-out of muck

like whac-a-bone.

a laborious battle through burlap sacks

and generations of shrubs.

toiling, trying to punch their way through.

the sky is a raven-black gravity dam,

the moon an eyelet,

the clouds are in hiding,

the time, a *dead watch*.

in no time, an organized battalion

of screw-faced bone soldiers march in formation.

trampling beer cans, chip bags and

scratched off lottery tickets,

on unkempt soil of boneyard.

which for decades have been untried,

until this grim night.

disremembered veterans of an unknown calvary,

are leading the way with rake feet;

underworld fled bondservants of yesteryear follow suit.

old man willis settles down across unfilled railroad tracks,

back-and-forthing in a whining rocking chair,

loosening floor board screws,

wiping prolix eyes like *"the hell is that?"*

completely bass-mouthed,

a half bottle of whisky goes to waste.

well, i'll be damned!

i guess even violence moves in silence.

never sleep on the quiet," says old man willis.

dust bunnies bouncing off the worn-away enwraps,

of all members with every single step.

nearby storefront window shatters into variant pieces.

everything is left intact; apart from a bothered unoccupied

pegboard wall.

the county fair is in town--

hot, buttery popcorn smell, donut elephant ears,

h*ope you have a dental plan* candied apples,

little horsey carrousel, rusted squeaky ferris wheel,

and of course, the doctored games.

townsfolk of dandysville are in for a rude

awakening on this gladdening night.

the sojourns from the mist wow the little ones,

frighten the living daylight out of seasoned heads,

as they parade down the streets in all bone

(which kids mistake for costume).

while marching they sang,

"i'm coming up, on the rough side of the mountain.

and i'm doing my best, to make it in."

the gang of soldiers leisurely approach the crowd,

gazing at them with the blankest stares in history.

highest rank of all generals march forth,

raises a picture of fort craig, nm., cemetery,

says to them, *"take us here. nowww!"*

cool as hell raptors

versus silent film basic black & white bubble tv dinosaurs

asked my mom last week if she was participating

in any of the upcoming juneteenth events

her reply, "when did june have a baby?"

'f' the pig who wears the blue uniform

and badge without honor & dignity

and trailer park rebel flag racist

who backhands his related wife

from stained carpet of his one room

living room bathroom kitchenette

& his uncaring privileged sister karen

they'd rather us be back on plantation fields

dying like roots & pokeweed plants

us cool as hell raptors versus them

silent film basic black & white bubble tv dinosaurs

we are a modern-day monster clash

kong versus godzilla or thrilla in manila or

recovering addicts versus the antidote dealers

we see life through inverted cat sunglasses

we have wrestled down sabertoothed tyrants

which is to include a gawt damn tyrannosaurus rex

shooting bow and arrows

then accusing us of putting hands on him like

roman catholic clergy

we aim to set our beautiful people of color free

of oppression and heal post-slavery scar tissue

rather than in shining armor we fight the fight

in decorated coverings and retro j's

the shiny ones with the 45 & icy semitransparent outsole

(to be precise)

and assorted masks for covid-19 protection

"we wear the mask!" it too grins, it too lies

like melpomene & thalia & dunbar we wear it well

we fight not only for our own liberation

as they say, *"you are not the victims here!"*

WE ARE THE VICTIMS HERE:

WE ARE BREONNA TAYLOR, WE ARE ATATIANA JEFFERSON,

WE ARE RAYSHARD BROOKS, WE ARE DANIEL PRUDE,

WE ARE GEORGE FLOYD, WE ARE AURA ROSSER,

WE ARE STEPHON CLARK, WE ARE BOTHAM JEAN,

WE ARE PHILANDO CASTILLE, WE ARE ALTON STERLING,

WE ARE MICHELLE CUSSEAUX, WE ARE FREDDIE GRAY,

WE ARE JANISHA FONVILLE, WE ARE ERIC GARNER,

WE ARE AKAI GURLEY, WE ARE GABRIELLA NEVAREZ,

WE ARE TAMIR RICE, WE ARE MICHAEL BROWN,

WE ARE TANISHA ANDERSON, WE ARE ELIJAH MCCLAIN.

we know their stories and their names

we know them well and there are more

we know there are more hidden and more to be found

as we continue our search for justice

i hope to sight the abdominal snowman

my plan is to offer him a dare t-shirt,

a stick of 48-hour deodorant, bacteria killing

mouthwash and skin care products

all in exchange for any antiques he

may have on his person

if i can get rich by tomorrow

i can solve a gargantuan poverty equation

i stand a better chance of finding that myth

along with offspring of the lochness monster

than we do in finding justice and equality

that is so america

i am on you like black on

black forbidden rice, said cletus to jerome

before jerome stopped running, turned around

pointed the blicky at his headcheese

same way liquor frizzles between virgin tonsils

hot metal melted like ice through skin

then through bone temple

how can a man kill his own cousin

for plucking a roup infected chicken?

i said to crenshaw

then we hit the fence right before cops

or medics arrived

remember, snitches wear master splinters!

says an intoxicated street alley prophet

as we breezed by running like locomotives

unfortunately, not fast enough to escape

the smell of dumpster juice and hard times

percolating from dirt layers

onioned *around* his body

to the guy telling me not to tattle

on the assassin who offed my childhood friend

that is so america

two of my blood brothers

already lost them to street wars

one at fifteen

the other at forty-one

to foolish boys of their color

foolish niggas *from around the way*

as medics waitressed their lifeless cadavers

i said to myself i bet in their eyes

our tar skin makes us appear as animal

yet will look at us as being inferior

to horned milk ram

to mulatto pandas

and sombrero tiger cats

we consume ourselves the same way

they consume us

same way they consume their people

and satan who is geriatric perverted

maggot food by now

spending its generations unrotting

back to life

in a straitjacket chained to ceiling

of an underground hitler bunker

gets to consume all who sneezes

at the commandments

for my two faraway brothers

who were innocent and unarmed

when tatted with infinite wounds

of gun violence

numbers and numbers of damn days

i have ripped page after damn page

silently healing then revealing

dark pain venomed inside this damn cage

like operating on a damn bed of nails

a heart inflated with red rage

stringing thread through

one hundred wounds

but *who is there to mend*

a heart balloon?

that is so america

as kids we partake in

preschool sandbox antics

our brains over time mold into

power stations for dreams

we raise crinkled avocado paper

and scream *"loyalty over these dead presidents"*

then we grow apart to grow into affiliated enemies

pretending to tolerate one another from distance

using each other for life-size measuring sticks

wondering, *how is there life compared to mine?*

that is so america

then there are the cops and wannabes

cattle-housing black unarmed bodies for slaughter

as if our lives were only worth

$1 in food stamp credit

which still may be enough to purchase

skittles or a can of watermelon fruit

juice cocktail

not to exceed value of a gun owned by a neighborhood

watch devil

which would likely go for $250,000 on an auction site

especially with a young black body on it

and i say again

they kill us and we kill ourselves

then they kill their people

so, when i am asked if i believe in

"black-on-black crime"

i respond by asking,

is a zebra black-on-black

or does white-on-white stripe?

they turn their nose hairs up knowing

that is so america

i have witnessed a brotha

wearing a kufi over *iverson cornrows*

get stereotyped by the cops

while walking with a *walkman*

in a predominantly black area

which is nothing out of the ordinary

array of *sun-stripe*

now had he been cuffed for wearing a kufi

while eating pork belly bacon

i'd have no gripes

white ghosts hiding behind blue uniform

assassins hidden behind smiles of friendship

murderers blending with the twilight

biggots hiding behind anything they can find

don't you fools know

if we do not wake heaven or hell

will snatch us from our sleep

if we ever get it together

we can get it, together

but we won't

that would not be America

god bless children of america

i love reading joy off of my

children's expressions

like an uncracked fresh fragranced soap

i am smelling for the first time

each day i return from a hard day's work

the way they hem me into the wall

with their little love

using my long legs for pillows

turning me into a weak praying mantis

and playing melodies to my soul

so when i think about the father

who has prematurely been

sent to his final resting place

i think about his child standing there

waiting and waiting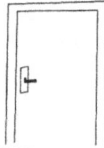

on his return

not knowing they will never

again see their father

walk through that door

maybe she learned a new word

can say "*dad*" for the first time

(a day too late)

maybe he crafted a beautiful picture

a sun, a little birdie, a rainbow and clouds

(signed "*for dad*")

a billabong of raging lunatic streams

out of my vision down my cheeks

knowing there is a child in this lake of tears

saying "*i can't breathe!*"

the worst of these cops and

the worst of these street niggaz

don't give a damn about us

don't give a damn about our kids

all windswept adolescent memories

never again to be gathered

to pieces

365 days of you (abcs of love)
for my wife christen

our hands match on fountain lake

as we set sail i deeply wonder

if we become submersible

what could outlast our glow of love

you are powerful and you are brilliant

and your spirit is of stunning beauty

no bother with fluctuating confidence

i am silver liquid metal chained

to your precious heart

understanding beyond grievance

greatest-woman-to-ever-walk-earth

you are without a shadow of doubt

like the sweetest bouquet

you bring color into my world

we can grow branches and branches

and branches together

rebirthing aboriginal great tribes

with likeness to pequot villages

first learn to always love yourself

i'll accept all you have left

only if you can walk

in your own light

while letting me lead

(everwanting you forevermore)

Small Talk at Dunn's Bottom

over a bologna sandwich & sanford & son

in a time travel machine

i'd go back as buzz aldrin

not for the purpose

of becoming an astronaut

but to be the very first

person in history

to put a foot in every

slave owner's moon-pie

over a rolling tray & langston hughes poems

what is a dream?

what is a vision?

when you allow power

of influence to be

greater than purpose.

it is someone else's…

"puff puff, pass!"

over mustard sardines and

late-night erectile dysfunction commercials

life is sardine-can fine caviar
enjoyed tasteful exquisite living
misleading into twisty-
faceted queer aftertaste
with rough whetted brim
of boundary

while riding its plane
do not get pricked

over eggs and rice and no electricity cheap candles

if being broke doesn't
move you to a place of
creativity
you will never make it

over live screening church and being born again

no one ever loses power

no one ever loses faith

we forget where it

comes from.

we forget who gave it to us.

DAMMIT! i forgot to pay the light bill!

let a string of violins wail for the kid
(farewell to elijah mcclain)

being possibly the most mournful day of many to uncrumple.

we the cool as hell raptors meet in a respectful place,

to say hello and goodbye to a perfect stranger.

my ears widen to conversation taking place near me.

"perhaps, murder, someday, will be considered a crime."

said the smart young raptor to the well-seasoned one,

who has lived long enough to see the same screenplay,

from black and white. to now, live and in living color.

hundreds of violins string majestic sound,

at washington square park.

we stand under shields of cloud as hopeless spectators.

ivory and charcoal swans synchronize-glide atop the coating

of the unnatural lake.

aged-hair colored squirrels munch on nuts

and nourish elderly trees.

we plank here, hiding upside-down smiles

and vibrating lips undermask.

for what sadly has become a typical occasion,

another embalming table holding another black bare body.

how dare anyone commit the crime of

wearing ski mask while black!!!

and the thugs who have taken his life

still roaming about, wild and free,

like bloodthirsty komodo dragons.

"it is a broken record in the sense

that the system repeatedly plays itself.

you'd think those badged to prevent crime,

wouldn't be the same people committing them.

when will it all end? who is there to stop it?

will the kid find justice in his sleep?"

said the well-seasoned raptor to the youngin'

as the police departs the harmless crowd,

to discontinue a peaceful resuscitation of life through tribute.

"we came. we paid homage.

we sent melodies to elijah, uncle art."

the smart youngin' said to the seasoned raptor,

as she put her arm around him and they both walked away.

visibly brown: our inductions for american history

we select david walker,

we select oluale kossala,

we select joseph w. winters,

we select robert f. fleming jr.,

we select nathan "nearest" green,

we select joseph cinque,

we select garrett morgan,

we select thomas martin,

we select leonard c. bailey,

we select george t. grant,

we select charles drew,

we select benjamin banneker,

we select frederick m. jones,

we select osbourne dorsey,

we select alexander miles,

we select aemilia bassano,

we select all 'black wall street' victims,

we select all 'red summer' victims,

we select all past-fled, past-bled "human cargo,"

we select future uncelebrated black america.

you all meet and have met the requirements.

you may find your rightful places

in the american history textbooks.

if black lives matter today,

let's make this matter...

21 guns salute

21 guns salute

another soldier died today

left the world destitute and lonesome

without a single flag on his grave

a shell-shocked vietnam vet

dishonorably stripped of his stripes

conned by the con-stitution

blighted during an unfortunate plight

ravaged by the republicans

devoured by the democrats

scraps left for the independents

the world's filled with aristo-rats

legs utterly amputated

while shedding red for the blue and white

slayer of numerous mercenaries

but diced in half by the katana of a dissipated life

the stars on his banner faintly shimmered

after battling, for what little he had left

given a purple heart half-heartedly

then an uphill battle

until he meets his very last breath

21 guns salute

for all homeless soldiers of past wars

another soldier died today

because life wasn't worth fighting for

matchbox stick (night over the winelight)

time ago,

monte carlo cruise

lone match met lonely strike

our eyes touched across the room,

a spark, that ignited 'in a flash'

we laughed and waltzed from afternoon,

becoming betrothed, in spite

of being a match, of being a strike,

a spark, that ignited 'in a flash'

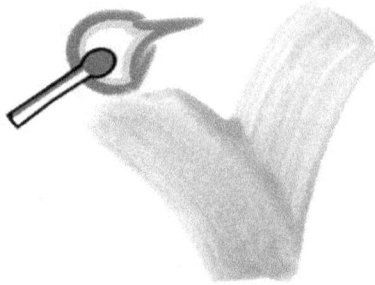

a truth deferred (after langston hughes)

how can i find a truth deferred?
does it tunnel through loam?
when no one is around.

does it bug like june beetles?
make hissing sounds.

does it inject viperous venom?
as it bedevils errin' souls.
or maybe it's just so fiendish,
'cause its blood is so damn cold.

maybe it slithers itself around,
while eking-in through the cracks
of your house.

or has it already escaped your mouth?

a dream withered (after langston hughes)

how does a dream get withered?

does it spin itself into a cocoon?

before turning into a butterfly & winging-a-way.

disappears into the old wild yonder?

camouflaging behind pink, orange, blue, or grey.

does it even try to find the runway?

travelling through a seemingly lackadaisical world.

or is it solely fixated on its own beauty?

the reflection in the lake causes its mind to swirl.

maybe it just puddles all day,

as it languidly sits on its behind.

or is even having a dream,

furthest thing from its mind?

the red light district

sarah,

works late into the night,

as if she had no other option(s)

day in and day out,

up and down the zona norte district, tijuana

like a traffic light fixed on green,

she works through

like grey poupon or bed sheets,

she lies down and spreads

like wildered raccoons who scour their viands

under waning crescent moons

and citrus-high lit noons

in flophouse rooms and fat cat venues,

the girl works nonstop--

as if cross-stitching in sweatshops

she works the customers till they tummy flop

a man-eating tri-sarah-tops

that sunksqua can loop and tom-a-hawk

whether it be iquana ranas mezal shots,

up and down the sliding poles

on the la coahulia beatstreets,

to *"mommy, please stay home!"*

what's life's purpose when love comes in modicums?

what when hearts chisel to naught,

via osteotomes?

this world is not one for itinerant peons

but she continues to work,

and no, she is not alone!

the world's blackest hippie

where did all the kind love children go?

everyone wants to sample this lemon rind question

no one has an expressionless answer to.

"freeloading psychopathic baby boomer."

"runaway peacenik, no real cause to go against the grain."

i've been labeled everything under the wicked sun, man,

but that is neither here nor there. new day, new age!

i was once in vibrant youth; free in mind, body, and spirit.

as a fruit loop lorikeet,

or flapping bat-roaming ornithopter.

with no co-gamer throttling my joystick,

turning deaf toward every call. on my cockpit radio.

one of america's "land of the free,"

"good for nothing" standstill refugees. they say!

of course, this was prior to may 22, 1972.

day i landed my very first gig, man.

the day was bubbling hot oats,

over a larva red burner. dancing heat!!!

after picking through my lumberjack shag,

brushing more teeth, than i have,

on went a blinding hand-dyed tee.

ocean blue crotch cutter bell-bottoms.

minutes into marching up main street,

my feet were stretchy gooey cheese pull.

a brand new ghetto blaster

saddle-fitted my left shoulder blade.

the bee gees high-pitched falsetto

sounded like a screaming llama:

"cause we're living. in a world of fools. breakin' us down.

when they all should let us be. we belong to you and me."

fred "the hammer" williamson had villainous endangering eyes,

falling into his sights meant experiencing a million deaths,

at once. street boys at the poolhall pitched pennies,

rolling dice all day.

hillside at donna's restaurant

had the best west african groundnut stew in town.

always bowl-sticking, thick and rich in flavor.

lightly-simmered zucchini kept its preserved crunchiness.

the godly aroma saturated clothing,

interrupting sense of smell throughout the day.

hottest day of the year, without a doubt.

thought the sun had fallen out of the sky

into the earth's thigh cushioning.

had more water streaming down my face

than the amazon river, man.

chucked up two bone digits.

in direction of hovering shagon wagons.

"peace to all" and "flower power,"

tatted over candy lace paint jobs.

had i forgotten more than i remember of this story,

life today would not have a new opened box of sneakers smell.

there is a darling of a woman who still resides on main street.

goes by the name miss retha. she had a mellifluous little voice.

when she organized bake sales, every household placed orders.

while walking along her house on this particular day,

her area-famous sweet potato pie and nut bread

showcased from the window seal. smoke signaling every starv-
ing insect

within a three-mile radius, more than tempted me to dive.

my fingers deep into a pie or two.

no one comes between a southern woman and her cooking.

would have carved me like a pumpkin, with a dull-edged
butcher's knife.

chickens defeathered themselves: bathed in large stock pots,

of chilled lemon pepper laced marinade. to keep cool.

that is how hot it was. fidgety boys literally flooded streets,

with uncorked fire hydrants. bouncy gals chalked numbered

squares,

on pavement for games of hopscotch: jumped rope with borrowed water hoses.

mister ice cream man profited so much, he hung his soda jerk hat for good.

had we known the history behind that watermelon song

he cowbell-called us with…. ughhhhhh!

how many more hidden-in-plain-sight lies are there left in the world to discover?

for all we know: the martians & moon-pea headed people

received their walking papers: a longtime ago.

after a brief stop to listen to "shirley with the afro puffs"-

storefront preach on righteous "power to the people" topics-

it was off to the races like a greyhound event.

reason behind my crusted eye travelling,

a beneficial interrogation, with not just anyone.

the most important man in all of d-town,

who has summoned me with an unclear mission.

a man of little small talk, who deserved no questioning.

the globe by then had reached gravitron spinning velocities.

me, sell my beloved soul? to make friends on wall street?

join a robotnik society? motivated by monetary gain.

not at all what i represent; then and now, man.

was not missing this opportunity for the world.

so, i bumped into a hottie;

one i had a crush on since school daze. a doll named christen!!!

sweet sticky starfruit maple tree fly mama. that's what she was.

attractive in every fragrance of the word. yes, she was!

just'a sashaying the block with her mama, missy gladys,

her hips beat wind from-side-to-side like a drum major.

when i saw them, on that steamy hot sunny day.

both clutched grocery bags in butter-tone cotton mitts,

"what's crackin' foxes?" i said to them.

"huh... child?" replied missy gladys (blushing).

i replied, *"can i help you two with those?"*

"sure, you can honey dumpling!" she responded.

christen looked on quietly.

i gave her a prod and a wink wink

as she surrendered her bags.

her lips, a bloomed delicate featherness

picked out of the bayou haystack.

a lonely breeze caught her polka-dotted sundress,

introducing her self-rising business underneath.

when her eyes collided with mine, in time,

i saw a special escapade awaiting us;

had ever we found one another. perhaps we could have.

battled this eyeclops hand-in-hand.

times were different: i was different: we were different.

we found her "welcome home" mat far too soon.

on my cheek's softest spot, she left a smudged lipstick imprint.

worn proudly on my face, until peeling with the week.

after all of which had taken place, a one lamp dinging dungeon,

in front of three unreliable shadows, was where i finally found myself.

a recognizable shape smiled at me with possum eyes

and razor tiger shark teeth.

from behind a sizeable compartmental desk

the other two stood to the left & right side of him.

they had no facial features but crab cracker claws.

when he told me to sign on the dotted line,

in my jittery hands, there was no hesitation.

my fire-lit, coal pit's wheelbarrow has trundled

tirelessly ever since.

awaiting the greatest war of salvation.

father, before your confessional i stand

with this most difficult conundrum:

matthew 7:16 asks the question,

"do people pick grapes from thorn bushes, or figs from thistles?"

if i wear an infrangible nutshell,

if i embody a saccharine soul,

where will the wedge in between eventually lead this man to?

at the end of every rainbow (uncle art & i)

one day, while gazing through an aperture in our window, i discovered a clandestine beauty that had never before been noticed until that day. every time it downpoured, an outpour of colored light always seemed to commence from the skies over the project buildings. it didn't pose long at all before going forth. it would always come and go like the yeti, with very few ever noticing it. people around deland have been through so much disbelief that their eyes will no longer allow them to see anything beyond. they are afraid to follow. taking after others have often led down a road with no outlet.

"imagination, sometimes, aids with flipping the script on certain situations. true, the sky may be the limit, but we're in a world with unlimited limitations." uncle art tells me this all the time.

i, myself, had never been the type to believe in things like fables or fairytales. what we discovered one day would change my mind. one early morning, uncle art and i decided to chase the end of that sky of colored light. being that he finally convinced me to take this journey,

i thought for sure we'd see the little lucky charms fella with the pointy ears and fancy belt buckle, or a huge pot of shiny valuable tokens! what i found that day was much more valuable than any past crossbone and skull scarf-wearing pirate treasure. darn-near half the neighborhood found out about our plans. some gave words of encouragement. others either raised red or yellow flags to cripple our progress. some even offered to give us lifts in gas guzzlers. unc was so quick to turn them away.

he said, *if we wish to make it to the end of that rainbow, it will have to be on our own power. there are no shortcuts in life, strength comes with experience. when we've seen and faced*

everything that this world has to offer, there isn't anything that
we should be afraid to go through.

he was absolutely right. on this journey alone, we were con-
fronted by at least four snakes, feet-blistering ground pebbles,
and a family of brown bears. after so many trips, stumbles, and
near collapses, we finally reached the stopping point.

unc: we're here pokey pine!

me: we're where?

unc: at rainbow's end, silly child.

me: you have got to be kidding me. there is nothing here.

unc: yes, there is. open your eyes kid. look a bit closer.

me: unc, i have 20/20 vision. if there was anything to see, i'd
see it.

unc: try opening your third eye kiddo.

if true prosperity could be seen with the naked eye.

don't you think everyone would find it?

me: very true. now what am i supposed to see again?

unc: do you see that sign over there?

me: you mean the town exit sign?

unc: yes. the town exit sign.

past that is where you will find your treasure chest.

were you expecting some pointy-eared fella with a

fancy belt buckle? i have some money i have been

saving since my marine days. take it and.......

me: no, unc, i refuse to leave you here with a family who

could care less about you.

unc: listen. if you want to take care of me, do so

by making the world a better place.

you cannot do that from a rinky dinky town.

you have what it takes to be a positive voice for the people.

to be that person, you have to be on that stage.

now call me soft or whatever. my eyes became a leaky faucet. not only did i inherit uncle art's savings of $2153, he gave me an aged hand glass, which had been passed down for generations. this gift allowed me to see an unforeseen attraction within my essence. immaculate bow of gorgeousness ribboning from within. money to build new life outside of the rundown. all these proved to be more valuable than anything imaginable.

with uncle's golden advice, i now have a firm belief, that there are endless opportunities at the end of every rainbow.

natural mystic garden (sankofa)

in the natural,

she waters her leafy garden.

her angel orchids. her coneflowers.

her snapdragon encloses a known

butterfly-fairy within its cushiony grasp,

to pour colorink within an everchanging

evanescent pottery wheel.

light reflects upon her harvest,

to illuminate its delicate core.

moongasm vibes orbits the cool smooth

breeze, to flower.

in the natural,

she waters her leafy garden.

breakdancing on the streets paved in hiphop

every floor ridden boombox's quake transfuses juice

through artery cracks of dilapidated urban concrete

giving us an impulse to become vibrant braeon mannequins

today's mumble rappers are said to be from the city of bab-
ble-on

us chucky taylor high top all-star b-boys slinky coiled

into unearthling-like movement

picture ghetto street mimes with hissy fit demeanors

& ohio players swag

working deeply fixed quick twitch muscles

ones never sought after by the common couch potato

although, breakers & couch potatoes do commonly connect

with one having an asset, the other being one

who did not want to be like both mikes?

and turbo & ozone in the 80s?

who would ever think to name a movie electric boogaloo?

turbo wore a zebra haired bruce leroy kung fu manchu bandan-
na,

outlining his jheri curl covered forehead like a fitted slap brace-
let.

his care bear tee & skintight karate gi bottom garnet.

what the kid did with a broomstick wiccan can only fantasize
about.

ozone wore the same hat mj probably wore in every video.

he sported costume jewelry,

which would have confused any jacking sparrow coasting
ashore.

his no sleeve leather button up vest gave his color cut & clarity.

a shaq foo shazam hoop circled his ear,

like an orca's family hunting demo.

no duo on the planet could ever match their moves,

not even the best two moonwalkers on or around earth.

mike jack & neo armstrong could not have topped that.

each on-the-dime move produced dimensional images.

double-jointed body bending acrobatic flash & crease.

on the rhythm of a funky beat.

most breakers danced tougher than they were.

the beat streets have since grown faint.

the sound of the instruments is different.

the rhythm & words are off-flow offbeat.

spirits of the breakers can still be caught,

ricocheting off dividers of thoroughfares.

in timeless aesthetic memories frozen in spray can

decorated layered blocks.

all are historic entities: all are paved prodigies,

of what we call old school hiphop.

the pool shootin' junkie

in 1963,

neshoba county, mississippi

fish grease colored café,

i saw the legendary pool shootin' junkie play

it happened after sunfall last sat-day

over yonder cross muddy creek

in the mist, by a cesspit

where a yella alligator sleeps

they'se a'fiddled & a'reeled

to sum fine crooned blues

they'se slurped shine

ate wautermelon

and thick gumbo stew

deep off in backwoods mississippi

where mosquitos hook like

bristle-faced catfishes

saw that man call all 'is shots

never once did i see's 'im miss

aimed 'is wooden elephant gun

'tween 'is oatmeal bridge

knocked one down

three went down

five hit the corner

then six....

only seconds after seven pocketed

eight bass-mouthed for a win

the pool shootin' junkie stormed off

sangin' a braggarts shout:

"folks come cross dah wauter

just'a yappin' they mouth

by the end o' the day

nothin' seems to come out

dey comes'a struttin' in the door

gals crowded around

by the end o' the night

they tryin' ta rub me down

i tell em, i am not a dog

so i do not hound

jus' da best pool shooter

ever played in this town!

i'se jus'a pool shootin' junkie

wit money on ma mind

if you take'a closa look

you'd see no fear in muh eyes

as your pockets runneth dry

mine'll steadily rise

if you left here broke

no one 'ould be surprised"

doubt any locals were surprised that night.

but if anyone happens to asks:

over yonder cross muddy creek

in the mist, by a cesspit

where a yella alligator sleeps

there is a legendary pool shootin' junkie

by the name of sam smitt

saw that man call all 'is shots

and never once did i see's 'im miss

aimed 'is wooden elephant gun

'tween 'is oatmeal bridge

life's slippery slopes

there is only so much
we can get away with in life
this temporary life we lead
has not a single favorite
fear brittle heart of no man
never trust a feeble mind
swathe a band around staying power
evading dreams you'll find in due time
hold onto life's slippery slopes
let nothing get in your way
enervate speed of evasive aspirations
by giving dreams your hope to see
for at least another day

life's slippery slopes

if a wishing well could wish

wells are often used for wishing,

but what happens when a well runs dry?

does the well's infelicity

cause the world to turn its back,

as it guzzles on the inundated windfall of the next?

will tears sympathetically downpour,

to fulfill the parchedness of the well,

instead of leaving it in neglect?

has the world frozen over completely,

with no sign of warmth?

so love is now too far-fetched.

the softness of their infirmed hearts have congealed,

leaving them with absolutely no regret.

if a wishing well could wish,

would the world find a way to make

its wishes come true?

because its very last wish would be to someday

find its inner strength inside of you.

if a wishing well could wish...

from the cot to the charnel
(a fish story)

sluice poison in the dirt for the silenced-foot soldiers

douse their dry-rotted bones with bottled heat

from the cradle to the grave they once towered then tumbled

buying lies every day from the weak

once lived a kingfish

he was thought to be honcho of the sea

kingfish had a little squirt

then got eaten trying to swim too deep

little squirt was left to swim alone

his father was a kingfish but he was gone

he got greedy tried to swim away from home

this tadpole thought it was safe to roam

with no schooling he had no tutelage

he saw hooked bate so he just looped it

those dangling worms

those seven-leaf clovers

life was a *waterloo*

his story's over

sluice poison in the water for the *silenced-foot* soldiers

douse those light fishbones with bottled heat

from the sea to the shore they once swam then stifled

buying lies every day from the sea

the epitaph (where we belong)

in the end,

while black, brown, blonde, or red

turns into white or grey,

our pearly whites

cringe up and all rot away.

our strong and young

turns into frail and old.

death's rattle takes its form

as our bodies turn cold.

our lives are complete,

our stories are told.

we're *boxed up* & shipped home,

where we belong.

i know a place where the dead don't die.
(for grandma elnora)

i know a place where the dead don't die.

it's where moths and love bugs aviate through the skies.

it has a honeycomb, heaven for all humble bees.

it's where the flowers *skyrocket* high as sequoia trees.

it's where infants don't cry, and golden agers don't die,

and all colorful fruit trees are a sight for sore eyes.

it's where *chu chu* trains don't have any drive.

it's where life has no end,

because death has no care,

where the king takes his throne,

blowing blessings through the air.

it's where everyone loves,

and where everyone cares.

it's where people don't tease,

and people don't jeer.

it's where all have been accepted,

never again will they be denied.

it's where god's son shines brightest,

as he blossoms amid clouds in the sky.

i know a place where the dead don't die.

colorful spatters on graffiti wall

life is like a tried and true felon,

there just isn't any tellin!

sidewinders could be your dawgs,

hard-nosed kats could be "would rats."

we sometimes bend over backwards

to get stabbed in our backs.

too much greed will bleed you.

shuck and jivers aren't real,

like ghosts, they're see-through.

life is a measureless lesson.

a pulse is the highest of blessings.

sex is a lethal weapon

if you strap with no protection.

"no sense in claiming to be crook,

when people look, you're halfway shook."

black and white can both be green.

snowbirds fly sky-high,

a snowbird is a dope fiend.

sinister can be the minister,

the collection plate can be for a hot date.

strong-arming for change makes no cents.

bias misdeeds are common denominators

behind the non-common-sensed.

who was josiah henson?

what's the dawn settlement?

if you know the answer to this,

the name uncle tom should be irrelevant.

what's the basis behind being racist?

the meek hold sole supremacy,

so segregationists could use facelifts.

there are heights some are afraid to reach.

lessons even teachers shouldn't teach,

certain contracts some should never breach.

if your arms are too short to box,

you may want to think outside the box.

creepy-crawlies turn beneficiaries

once we reach the cemetery.

a migraine is a belch to the insane.

chatterboxes have jam-packed brains,

and i heard that through the grapevine,

from a tree full of lemons and limes.

word of mouth comes bittersweet,

so pick and choose ripe words to eat.

life to some is but a dream,

when their way of living is unparallel.

ever seen a man-at-arms with no arms?

ever seen a rock crab with no shell?

have you ever seen a grabby ex-president?

a cephalopod who helmed a pirate ship?

ever heard of douglass, tubman, malcolm, mlk?

for freedom to be free today,

someone's life had to pay our way.

rainbows long have thrown up peace signs,

in a world that can never cross a ~~line~~

because we're too colorblind.

today is tomorrow.

let us bring yesterday to an end.

love eclipses multitudes of the most hateful sins.

now ask yourself:

am i willing to die for my kith & kin?

where sadistic ogress' rule the land

annihilated from earthly existence,
planted beneath an ersatz tumulus.

flesh devoured and torn to shreds,
soul grubbed out from beneath the ground.

a puppet of implausible gravitation,
impeded by disbelief, as it miraculously astounds.

elevated by the squalls of a blizzard,
throttled by the graupel of salivating clouds.

hurled into the crawlway of the brown of dusk,
tightly squelched where intricate in sight and sound.

digested down into a mysterious but uncluttered land,
where sadistic ogress' pilfered rule from misogynistic men.

jack johnson is hero

if loving is what i am guilty of

go ahead please convict me.

shackle me up

lock me away

chastise me.

deface the memory of my legacy

mark me utterly out of misery

strip me of my golden victory

i am the greatest fighter in history

so make sure you throw away

the skeleton key

whatever the case,

i'll still be free.

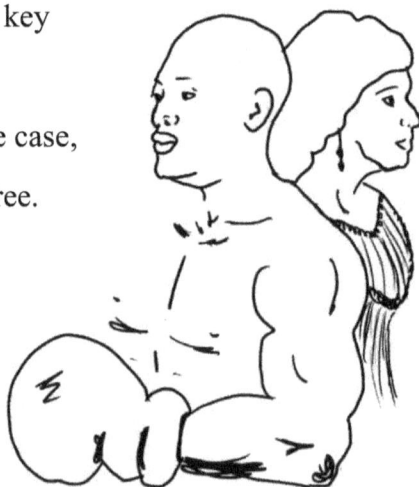

E.D. SMALL

like a quiet storm brewing

mr. barry white had the voice of a quiet

storm brewing. like a mug of steamy

whipped chai tea and late-night radio

voice of choice. an appalachian brown

cocoa liquor, cocoa butter sugar hill.

oil slick blackberry brillo-beard

laid by carpentry.

hand saw. claw hammers. chisels.

fingerwaves were pressed gypsum

sand dunes. if i thought anyone looked

like jesus, he would bare resemblance.

his performance was on high demand

like a southern bcu marching band.

we came to burn this mothership down!

he singed:

won't be no stopping
all the discotheques
better be ready
we're gonna hit'em hard
hard and heavy
party strong
all night long

i am quite trusting

but had i been a cop bumping heads

with mr. white during the 1965 watts riots,

as he marched the streets for racial equality,

orchestrating love unlimited for his

brothas and sistas of color,

from days of riot,

to the rest of my days,

i would have had to watch

my woman,

even with my eyes closed.

foyer within hell's gates

as you make your entrance, be very timorous,

for i may just be the foyer within hell's gates.

beg for your life and throttle my door's protuberance,

just don't be baffled if you're burnt at the stake.

my walls sweat profusely from the incessant heat,

hydraulic pressure erects the inner walls of my bubbling skin.

an ocean of insanity muddles down to the core of my feet,

melting flesh travels down to the dock of my chin.

unsolicited kryptonite to hearts contrary to meek,

my voice is unheard to all trespassers.

the ear-piercing decibels of my stillness speaks,

once your soul has been halted by the slant of my horns.

you're going to wish to god that you'd never been born,

a life filled with misdeed has led you to my inferno.

good morning, salutations, and welcome home.

beg for your life and throttle my door's protuberance,

just don't be baffled if you're burnt at the stake.

as you make your entrance, be very timorous,

for i may just be the foyer within hell's gates.

a plaudit for your motherhood
for my mother retha

the motherly love you possess,

is blessed by god, it is divine.

the motherly love you possess,

more fruitful than a concord grapevine.

pure like the richness of caramel honey,

more lustrous than liquid glittery white gold.

your motherly love speaks in infinite tongues,

hugs & kisses plus a trillion hundredfold.

forever your children are indebted to you.

with our honor we shall always bestow.

this is a plaudit for your motherhood,

simply for allowing your seeds to grow.

eating spam & oreo and drinking thunderbird (three haikus)

eating spam

just received a call:

caller id: scam likely.

"damn bill collectors!"

oreo

home run. long distance

out of stadium, into

living room. sosa.

drinking thunderbird

the dry night capped off,

a bird soared, dropped melodies,

woke hungover sun.

the home front (not home to me)

high five me at the entrance door,

put a *big* smile on your face.

offer the portal of time skeleton key,

i would still feel out of place.

travel seven wonders of the world,

cruise emerald waters of distant seas.

you could even take me to a place,

where money grows like edible leaves.

i have come to a conclusion,

and it is one that i believe.

this place you call home,

is not home to me.

some come looking to find their place.

my time's far too precious to go to waste,

our hair goes from different colors,

to a blemishing white or gray.

we are juddered in our rockers,

we are driven to our graves.

bodies subside within earth's soil,

E.D. SMALL

our spirits are casted away.
all of this has led me to say...

i have come to a conclusion,
and it is one that i believe.
this place you call home,
is not home to me.

running (after gil scott-heron)

today, i decided to run-a-way.

i do not know exactly where away is,

so it has taken me all day

was hoping it had a decent place to stay,

does it have a leather couch

or a comfortable bed?

does it have a colored television?

will it prune me, clothe me, and keep me fed?

already seems like running away

wasn't a clever move.

people call me a nobody

'cause i've dropped out of school.

i'm disobedient

'cause running away has no rules.

you can just run away

and do whatever you choose.

it's too late to go back home,

i'd be looked at like a fool.

i've been running for far too long,

and i'm not on my own.

people run away to find themselves,

when all hope has gone.

i thought i was running for shelter,

but what does it mean to run for cover?

maybe i'm just evading annoyance

i've brought to my mother,

will i find away?

who's to say?

it was either run

or pop the blackhead on the gun.

was it smart to abscond?

i guess i'll find that out in the long run.

red in her eyes

can i go a day without seeing my mother cry?

it dismantles my heart to see that red in her eyes.

biting the same hands that once cradled me in,

as she'd sing those lovable lullabies.

i've done so much dirt that it may be hard to rectify,

it may be hard to come to terms with this,

but i won't know unless i try.

lord, will i live before i die?

will i live before i die?

will my father ever look me face to face?

looking into my eyes would sadly take him

to an all too familiar place.

he never stands to face his problems,

he'd rather bundle himself in fear,

knowing that if i ever failed,

it would be all because of him

never being that true father.

always on the roll like a stone,

always giving more love to the streets

than his own family at home.

then again, it is already too late,

that drifter is long gone.

he got himself gunned down,

suspect unknown.

he lived life too fast

to even think about living long.

can i go a day without seeing my mother cry?

it dismantles my heart to see that red in her eyes.

biting the same hands that once cradled me in,

as she'd sing those lovable lullabies.

i've done so much dirt that it may be hard to rectify,

it may be hard to come to terms with this,

but i won't know unless i try.

lord, will i live before i die?

will i live before i die?

on the rocks, with a chaser

as ground turns bottom up,
sidewinders turn backsliders.
in the mist of their puzzlement,
once bygone deceivers
mold into crackerjack pathfinders.

from our jejune love on the rocks;
to a chaser more appeasing to my palate.
any potion with an urge to want a chaser,
no longer has its favorable taste.

whirlwind pyramid

plummeted like an anvil

from the highest landform,

whirl-pooled into the downdraft

of the most atrocious seas.

entrenched within the clay of the earth,

by the mighty hands of god.

ashes blown into my face

by the flurry of the breeze,

preyed upon by the beasts of prey.

belly up on their endeavors

to fulfill their baneful deeds,

discharged from the clouds of hope.

captured by the arms of grace,

blindly led to the doors of freedom.

unexpected jolt to the face,

praised for astonishing feats.

given the liberty to march,

legs *bashed in* at the knees.

suffered through pains and aches,

belittled for slight mistakes.

ecstatic because heaven awaits,

stripped of all that was given.

non-repentantly got very livid,

shackled away and imprisoned.

now, a precious life's diminishing,

in a world where love is regrettably limited,

and hatred is sadly a necessity.

now, i humbly wear my heart on my sleeve,

undoubtedly, the lord is protecting me,

so, have at it by all means!

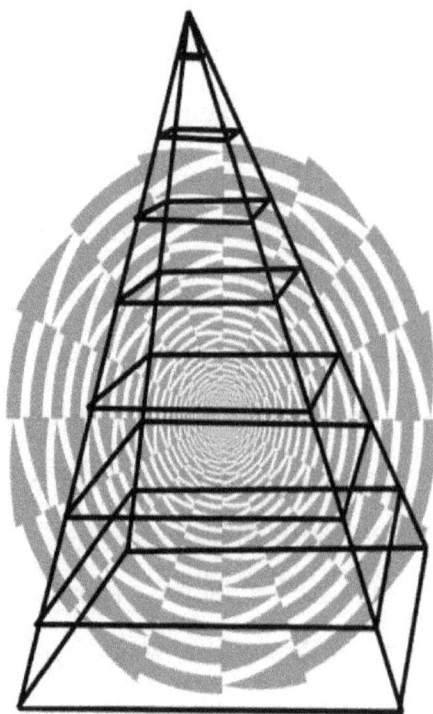

feel good jokes for donkeys

you are such a thoroughbred,

who put elf ears on your head?

bean thread noodles braid your face,

who gave you a belly-waist?

jerky legs are stiff as bark,

gallop laps to free those hocks.

stubborn mule come out that shell,

thumbtacked bush from pin-the-tail.

ain't no need to gawk this way,

go munch away on alfalfa hay.

no more jokes,

i'm such disgrace.

horse head! horse head!

what's with the long face?

christmuss story in the ghetto

all impecunious christmusses I recall

never involved a reindeer at all

some christmusses were so hard

santa came in a lawsuit

stocking stuffers were hung

on the wall in elf boots

grandma's fruitcake so brittle

today i lost my last tooth

santa came in a taxi

would have caved the roof

no hickory smoked turkey

or sweet honey baked ham

delighted in collard greens

with lardy pineapple spam

decked our door with a tire

which we used for a wreath

popo's sirens chased robbers

always kept us from sleep

entire ghetto went broke

when jack frost came down south

rather than glittering snow

he froze credit accounts

yet every christmuss got gifts

they delivered on time

bikes and remote control cars

such delightful surprise

but with each christmuss came storm

like drumsticks thudding our rooftop

drip, drop, drip, drop

or were they songs by 2pac

jesus saves

southern dewdrops cry down my window

slowly exposing a new array of opportunity

and good or bad promises day may bring

turning my eyes toward the clouds

looking for signs of heaven

jesus surfing condensed water vapors

with a surfboard branded *made in heaven*

scooping his chosen children

like a million scoop ice cream sundae

on a sanctified sunday

but leaving behind all kitty litter

in his baritone voice giving the greatest

motivational war speech ever heard

any man who is overly possessive of

this country has better be prepared

to burn and ash with it

with the latest trending life-taking malady

sending us one-by-one lord knows where

we can only bow & pray toward the east

everyday for the rest of our lives

in hope we someday get to meet natural causes

don't forget about god

don't forget which way is up

call me old-fashioned but I still believe in jesus

sometimes i feel like mike

sometimes i roll out of bed

feeling like my day will reflect

a mj 50-point-night

when the goals have changed in size

but suddenly seems impossible to miss

this providing a kick in the butt

into my work week

with my own size 17 sneakers

more than likely on a wednesday

putting me in the mindset

i will achieve everything

those haters said i cannot achieve

on those days when i have the mj bullseye

i won't be denied even if i am denied

after a day when i was *on fire*

while experiencing a day from hell

i constantly remind myself:

every one-hit wonder

Is always a shooting star

sometimes i feel like mike

sometimes i don't

honey butter slides

this restless mess-of-a-life is to dread

like braided rastafarian mopheads

bee skep and turban-hived

stiffened through beeswax of elemented time

soundtrack of nature vocalizing in forestry dark silence

aroused crickets commence to scream at an unseen presence

like a blind piano man *rhythm and blueser*

playing to incite excitement of a crowd of boozers

torrential pores of melted honey butter

sliding the wrinkled covering of tree skin

setting the dressing slab of the stage of age

a once in a lifetime song

drone's midair of a sold-out colony

streaming my curved antennas

"FINALLY, it is my turn to woo the queen!"

last words spoken of a falling *bee-leaf*

some bridges are not meant for crossing

from a lonely dark room

watching a social media clip

i witnessed several caucasian kids

push an "african american" princess

up a wealthy-looking neighborhood

in a little red wagon

chanting

black lives matter, black lives matter…!

instantly carving a graceful u

into my monday morning groggy expression

i bet dr. martin luther king jr. would

be ecstatically proud to see his dream

in spurts, travel as light through dark clouds

like bright bulb light to punctured lamp skin

if we just lie down and die

who will pay reparations on our souls?

if anyone, i bet these kids would

entrepreneur a lemonade stand

to balance america's greatest debt

if i could change the world

i'd do it from afar

in a world where stars shine

but nobody's a star

thinking back on impoverished childhood

when my mind was innocent and benevolent

socially withdrawn but positively charismatic

when kitchen lights were on before sunlight

ma flipping crusted edge skillet flapjacks

stacking them as high as ceiling's surface

cracking eggshell after eggshell after eggshell

donna, michelle, kendall, love, dontay

breakfast is ready y'all!

each week young carefree bear cub legs

took me to the local corner store

in less than two minutes (yes, i wore my stopwatch)

all of my allowance was swallowed

by *ms. pacman's* money hungry mouth

8 quarters can go a longway

especially on a stormy day

being that i wasn't the best at

those arcade games

i would sequester myself

until everyone had left the room

all except the on-duty cashier

looking on as if they were interested

in whether or not i earned a high score

my thoughts were so innocent as a child

then this happened...

if i could change the world

i'd do it from afar

in a world where stars shine

but nobody's a star

i travelled by foot

down the avenues of deland

a day prior to the *fourth of july*

in search of a licensed or unlicensed barber

my crown was in desperate need

of a fresh cut

fighting downtown tourist traffic

dodging hurried cars that probably

weren't going any-damn-where

souped up scorching jalapenos

& 16-wheel monsters

only to name a couple

appearing out of nowhere

in a tiny plaza i spotted a *grand opening*

i remember being so amazed at the

red, white & blue barber pole

thought it was the world's biggest peppermint

being a boy of my complexion

in a redneck crowded city

people watching was my forte

i laid off in the cut like dandruff

never saw a flake of darkness

enter that shop

enough is enough!

is what i told myself

i boldly walked the brand new walkway

there was no splattered gum

not a single crack to see with naked eye

as i swung open the saloon doors

like a scene from an old western

reduced clouds of dust particles cleared to

reveal three caucasian males & one asian guy

giving me *the cowboy stranger in town look*

just a second after i heard them laughing

their lungs out

right as i was making entrance

one of them being the barber

who was a grey haired elder caucasian

had to be every bit of 70 years old

he found his shaky voice before my

air flight 89s could touch down on carpet

wh-wh-what are you here for?

he stuttered

a bald h-h-h…….!

i uttered before rudely being cutoff

i d-d-don't do those here!

he said in an agitated voice

at nine years old i was confronted with

a torment that left me gathering myself

being hated for being black

i was heated, melting & wanted to repaint

his canvas rose red

along with every man who did not stand

up for me that day

if i could change the world

i'd do it from afar

in a world where stars shine

but nobody's a star

years after a bitter old man with a heart of hatred

nearly tainted my innocence

kind-hearted kids in the same skin

pushed a black girl in a red wagon

knowing

a shiny pearl can form

from a tiny grain of dirt

bringing me to the realization that

where there doesn't appear to be a path

there is still hope for some of us

to paddle against the tides of time together

some of us grow to respect others

for their differences

some are worm infested to the bitter core

there is no harvesting rotten apples

some of us want to live

while others will do anything including kill

to own a country they will never again own

two things that can't relate can never bridge

some bridges are not meant for crossing

BLACK HISTORY MONTH DRAWINGS
BY THE STUDENTS OF
T.O.P. ACADEMY

School name: T.O.P Academy (In DeLand, Florida)

Brittany Westberry, 8th Grade, Keith Cain III, 7th grade

Chelden Williams, 5th grade, Sariyah Lewis, 7th grade

Deyanna Pressley, 8th grade, RaeAnna Hill, 5th Grade

RaKail Hill, 7th grade, Richelle Hill, 5th grade

Deahn Pressley, 5th grade

Markesha James, Teacher

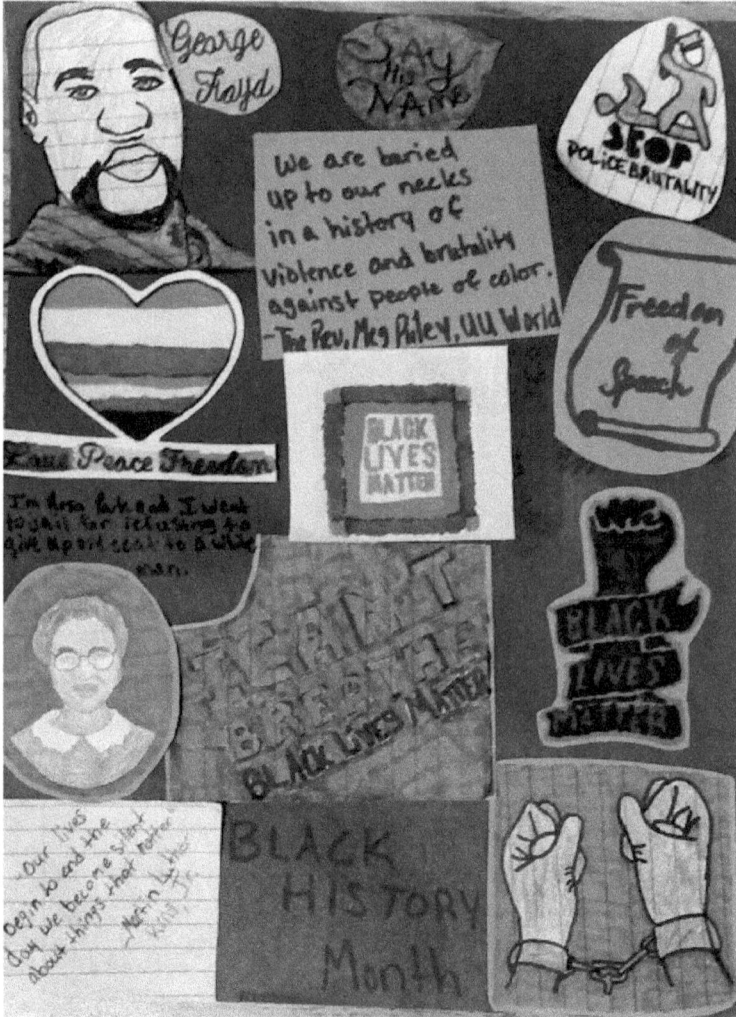

No Justice!!
No Peace!!
HANDS UP
This is a movement not a Moment
White feelings should never be held in higher regard than black lives
-Rachel Cargle
DON'T SHOOT
When the color of Skin is seen as a weapon you will never be seen as UNARMED!
I can't breath
Black Lives Matter

Macon Bolling Allen was the first black lawyer, argue before a jury, and hold a judicial position in the United States
James
MADAM CJ WALKER BEAUTY CULTURE
Madam CJ Walker Was recorded as the first female self made millionaire in America in the Guinness Book of World Records
"Our lives began to end the day we become silent about things that matter." -MLK
Jackie Robinson became the first African American to play in Major League Baseball in the Modern era
42
BLACK HISTORY

BLACK
Have faith like M.L.King
Innovate like G.W.Carver
Sing like Whitrey
Teach like Booked.T.W.
Overcome like Harriet Tubman
Run like Jesse Owens
Yearn for truth like Malcolm
LOVE
PEOPLE

BLACK Lives MATTER
I have a dream
August 28
1963
BLACK History MONTH

Black History Month
Black
Inventers/
famous
people

Black History Month
Hands up dont shoot
BLACK
LIVES
MATTER
JUST US
FOR
JUSTICE

about the author (the given definition)

what am i? i am swarthy-skinned.

my shadow is light.

i am the strength of my penumbra.

i am the buckler of my knight.

my heart bleeds red; i'm melancholy.

technically, my heart bleeds blue.

i epitomize what i'd call a bottom dog.

i am the given definition of the truth.

i am extremely well-rounded,

yet i am rough around the edge.

my mind isn't fully intact.

a poor porch boy with no arms or legs

strums a banjo with a bloody nub

inside of my head.

i am a son to my mother,

i have been a son of my sister's.

my mom is a daughter of her mother,

but poison once fathered her system.

my mind is frozen inside of icebergs,

and purified before thawing out.

so if you crave distilled knowledge,

sup smart water from my mouth.

i am a husband to my wife,

she is a sister to her sisters.

she is my bay-bee;

i am her mister twister.

i cyclone nectar toward the apple of my eyes;

she spittles honey by the border of my river.

i am not a buffalo soldier,

i am a soldier by default.

i am not of navajo descent,

i have not walked the long walk.

i've never lived on elm street,

kruegar has yet to slash my dreams.

a golden spear reflects off my beam,

please do not call me mr. clean.

you can call me dolemite,

i am not rudy ray moore.

my body's round & sugar candy coated.

my harvest is rotten to the core.

i've never played in the snow,

don't have the skills of len bias.

when people offer us that free base,

it does not mean that we should strike it.

i am not mr. tyler perry,

yet you can find me in a house of pain.

no grooves or moves like james brown.

no "talkin loud and sayin nothin,"

i have never rushed to see limbaugh,

and o'reilly was not a factor.

was no imus in the morning;

he went blind fury like the actor

(**rutger** haur).

who i am is who i am.

what i am is what you cannot see.

the odds that we all defy,

are the given definition,

of whatever we are supposed to be.

memoirs on a fundamental past bruthahood sistahood (part one: deland project housing pail kidz)

no one has ever tossed shoes over a powerline

without having a belief, they would someday return.

to find only a part of them still stuck in place.

our long-gone cuticles remember the wwf somersaults,

on bouncy gutted copper-colored urine-stained mattresses.

popcorn cotton bulging through worn-thin cloth with each pounce.

faces buried in someone's every night wet-the-bed mistakes.

that stigma we would have to wear through development.

we were livin' how we learned

in the city of deland.

sandlot days we skewer-spent in a southern heat,

on the field of sunflower seed hulls.

that is not what it was called; that is exactly what it was.

shells later became claw-mouth worker & drone canopy tents.

that thrown, laced, pigskin flailed the polluted air daily.

moving like a flying saucer,

houston oiled "air mcnair" firefly!

crashing into ten digit, receiving landing strips,

and tucked away faster than a government finding.

once you have seen rock-bottom from the bottom up,

you've centipede-twirled an ant farm labyrinth dugout.

where were most of our vanishing fathers?

it's funny, my friends and i never asked that question.

rumor has it, my father sent a baseball 400 feet.

we have never played a single game of catch.

we were livin' how we learned,

in the city of deland.

broken-winged bumblebees parachuting from

flower-head to flower-head.

that is what we were.

i remember my bros and i racing at the park:

rain, hail, sun, or even more sun!

we have heard rumors;

it once snowed in deland.

in deland, we have never seen it snow.

we ran within white-stenciled boundary hardcourts.

drained rim-stingy air-filled rocks from long range.

throwed down something thunderous,

lj "grandmama" style.

if the projects had a sponsor,

we would have been globetrotting.

like wilt. like meadowlark. like connie.

we should have had striking appearances

on garbage pailish kids sticker cards.

i remember all these names like yesterday.

i can recollect the names before the nicknames.

my hoodligans for life and whatever comes after life.

we gave the projects a generation with

a glittering dim star future.

had we come from a place with a big name,

people would today recognize who we are.

my cousins – montrale, johnny, and cab –

we would tangle with coral snakes for one another.

50 dudes chased three of my brothers and i

with red-on-yellow cue sticks.

there were no other underdeveloped blacks

in the movie mall that night.

only four black colors in a rubik's cube,

did not stick around to get twisted

and bent out of formation.

we ran together. so, we ran (together).

our legs were the most historic stampede.

no robbing folks. no killings.

no foolish stuff. we did not move too silly.

we were livin' how we learned,

in the city of deland.

where worms rest, we hid crated eggs.

close to the most ghoulish night of each year,

would toss dwight gooden fastballs over the hill.

left cars swerving from lane to lane.

rotted yoke does not remove easily from windshields,

i am sure of it.

my brother, kendall, crafted perfect cannons.

he made them with used evaporated milk cans.

they were loud enough to reroute an armadillo.

every hood has a cop who creates batman captions.

"smack" "wham" "bam" "pow" 'ouch"

we had a black cop we called *"super nig,"*

people avoided him like morning offering.

"shhh, be quiet! no tattle telling!"

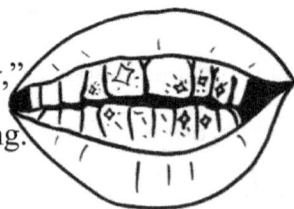

was one of our first childhood lessons.

also, our surest method of continued existence.

if we are still here, i'm guessing we listened.

we were livin' how we learned

in the city of deland.

"dem churen are bad as hell!
whose churen are those?"

"girl, did you get a visit from
the witnesses this mornin?
bushwhacked my damn door
till it splintered!"

"of all the wonders of the world...
just wonderin' why these people
keep throwin' fumigation tents
over these buildings?
damn roaches get pissed and come back
ten times stronger every time!"

"so, i was babysittin' tameka's baby the other day.
child, that baby run through more diapers
than the senior citizens' track & field team."
brought to you by our gossiping oldheads,

in a segment of "porch talk"

most days didn't have one bronze cent to our names.

nothing to shell-out to the sherbet lady.

or is it sorbet or flip lady (you choose)?

her yummy zip-sealed bumpyskin green pickles,

sunflower-shaped butter cookies,

bitter, utterly gross, pickled pigs' feet,

fifty cents assorted flavored sodas- from a dozen box

she purchased at the store for only three dollars.

our little spice apple town, quietly birthed entrepreneurs.

my compadres and i flew over to the breadbox bakery

after first ding of the schoolhouse bell every weekday.

that place had a bear-sized pit bull monster,

shackled to meager fencing outback,

spent its days yapping in disagreement

over daily mush-served-slop.

bet anything, he turned us into mouthwatering hambone

in his thought clouds. crazy, how assorted big boy treats

miraculously vanished from bakery shelves.

not sure how that happened? fingers, of course, pointed at us

and our little sticky fingers.

some of my peeps are the reason doors latch.

we were "always into somethin" like nwa.

130

most of my bruthas' were uncared for.

brown-green pears basking in the breadbasket of the beast

with stems slightly askew.

skint knuckle to skint knuckle combats.

carjacked alpine stereos.

"you know anybody who need hubcaps bruh?"
"know anyone who wanna buy food stamps?"

"which dvd would you like?
this one has an oscar buzz!
it's in the theaters right now!"

none of my dawgs ever let me down!

other than the time i bought that alleged

movie with an *"oscar buzz"*,

which went straight to dvd following week.

the critics didn't review it.

hell, i doubt if they knew about it.

probably would have slept through it (like i did).

and why am i seeing people get up?

to go get popcorn on this poor-quality bootleg.

regardless, i loved my bruthas-

had all the essentials needed to carry us through our days.

131

we were livin' how we learned

in the city of deland.

that disreputable stuff we are hated for, we glorify.

if the cheap haircut man screwed your head up,

you got laughed at all the way home.

had the best comedians i've ever witnessed.

with no credentials, one of my mute bruthas.

he was a bone-bruising silent nightmare,

"it is the quiet ones you always have to watch."

once again says our gossiping oldheads,

is not much to really speak on about him.

we were the creation of his moments.

we cradled what his surroundings feared.

when we left, the thistle lost compassion,

no one knows where a madman's mind travels

when his wits reach early retirement.

it came undone. link, by link, by link, unlinked.

eventually, every buffalo abandons his pack.

futuristically speaking, we all quantum-leap

into life declining easement. some futures come sooner than others.

we were not, and are not, perfect. we are, and were still, only human.

"how come no one ever makes it out of deland?"

heard this question a million times: never once believed it.

we are told, the way we entered the world

is the same way we make our departure.

we were told these bushy lies: my bruthas, sistas, and i made it out.

not together, but we made it. not all of us, but we made it.

not out of deland, out of youth. we survived the times.

as & past young & stoopid. good times, bad times.

we outlasted every one of those,

and we own every key to the city of survival

in the city of deland.

in dedication to my bruthas & sistas:

montrale. rod. r.j. damien & jennifer dunn. debo.

denise wright. roy & esha. nick nick. willie & mary.

the birch's: johnny. cab. tee. shinell. aaron thompson

julia & jay. adam. kentrell & kentrell. shantae.

octriss. kenneth. james & james. jerome.

jacquesta. victor. antwann & kc & Antwan gibson.

peter. renee & len. shayla. tommy lee & "pooh man"

anita. april. nuke. yvonne. deja. sean & breanna jordan.

the goosbys: junior, raynesha, & willie "little man"

terrell "pooh bear" darby. dirty duke. chris "beep" jackson

dee & dee. darryl thomas & darryl taylor & jo gunn

little terrell. donald & persephone. nitah & catoya

reggie & reggie. crystal & crystal.

rodney & richard & bopeete. dooley.

johnny & deandre & avoy. ballie & "big dawg".

lemeo. tymann. pacman. fats & damien.

chris & bowlegged lou. mann & cam.

disa burns-smith. boss (rip).

barbara. shay. pastor kevin.

memoirs on a fundamental past bruthahood sistahood
(part two: great urban american outdoor southern cookouts)

a zippy, buzzing house-fly zigzags from pillar to post,

making his untimely release from the free winds.

trailing a nearby viewless passage of sundry scents,

eventually settling on a red gingham farmhouse table.

to extend gestures with mister oglesby, the family fly swatter.

when it comes to potlucks, my family has four simple rules:

1. do not eat anyone's food unless you know them.

2. if you know them, make sure you <u>know</u> they don't have roaches.

3. if they own a cat, hell no!!!

if they own anything you'd kidnap from the zoo…

in the name of late great bishop bullwinkle,

"hell to the naw naw!"

4. just stay home and eat a bowl of scrambled eggs & rice!

memories of southern backyard family get-togethers.

ma and grandma's in-kitchen comedic monologue exchanges.

picasso-like handmade masterpieces catered on canvas plates.

sheets of chimney smoked turkey, over a bed of diced

gizzard-filled homemade dressing, chitlins, pigtail mustard

greens, potato salad, fried cornbread, macaroni & cheese,

candied yams. apple jelly cake. strawberry icing cake.

lemon cake. chocolate cake. vanilla frost cake. sweet potato pie.

"you name it!" a deviled egg without a sprinkle of paprika on top,

is usually water in the far-off desert for me.

i do not trust what i see. yuck!

all undomesticated game meats we monitored closely.

roasted possum, gravy smothered wild rabbit & veal,

and whatever preparations involved in raccoon cooking. ewww!

 leave the guesswork to the next family.

we needed to know in which saucepans they were tucked away.

they needed to be distanced from every other dish.

ma and young sis were the only ones who ate that nontraditional stuff.

what would a cookout be without this?

a gently basted, molasses sweet, trillionaire-rich bbq triceratops.

now, i am not sure how appetizing a dinosaur would be.

people would probably make it taste like chicken

(like they do with gator meat).

one thing i know, when it comes to bbq chicken and ribs,

bro-in-law wear's a gold crown; tighter than a kangol bucket hat!!!

in the city of deland.

as a matter of fact, i will be bold enough to state:

in a cook-off, my family on a fake plastic stove

(your family can have a real one).

my family still brings home the pesos.

no shame in showing up at cookouts unannounced.

"how did my friends get here? where did they come from?"

i am no trekkie, but i am a firm believer in teleportation.

we are all brackets from the same family tree.

it's all good in the neighborhood!

in the city of deland,

2 live crew. 69 boys. jam pony express. geto boyz.

trick daddy dollars. the poison clan.

a side & b side cassette tapes. had the neighbors' walls vibrat-
ing.

what some referred to as being "sexually explicit and misogy-
nistic,"

was referred to by us, as classic dirty south oatmeal milk booty
shaking.

we, obviously, played this away from grandma's ears (duh!).

none of our churchgoing aunts & uncles were in atten*dance*.

my youngest sister, she was always the life of the party.

all it took was a cabbage patch dance,

to make my cousins & auntie "act a donkey"!

we raced in the middle of the road. winner received $1 bragging rights.

although i vowed to take this to my grave,

my sister has always been a step, or two faster (than me).

phew! ok, i said it. some people don't get credit,

until they're buried in debt. after grandma packed and saddled,

her overnight bag for the land of milk & honey.

my oldest sis & bro-in-law, have been the family drawbridge.

"i am a real american. fight for the rights of every man."

since my heroes usually let me down.

do weird stuff like. get exposed as racists.

it makes me think unrelated thoughts like:

before i depart for the skies,

jolly rancher, please make new flavors!

and sly, can i get a sequel to "cobra" please?

i leave my loyalty in my unfailing family tree.

when we let each other down.

there is always someone there- to hold us.

in the city of deland.

Red City Boy's Travels to Can Crush
(Grime Doesn't Glitter like Gold)

A macadamia owl songbird hoots from a deeply tentacle-rooted
treehouse,
while I peddle up the block with a reused garbage bag full of
tin cans, thrown over my shoulder like a skunky mobile ginkgo
tree.
Back of my shirt and shorts drenched with rotted beer smell,
Cockroach eyes peep out like neighborhood watch.
My friends are outside playing games in the streets—where
they are supposed to be, at the wrong damn time.
Like the days I must scamper out the back screened door,
With a duffle bag full of empty gallon jugs.
It is never an easy task to remain unnoticed.
My chubby body withstands a lot of bumps and bruising-
I'm talkin' all-out combat simulation boo-boos.
I was lucky enough to avoid stirring up
Miss Lauren's chicken coup, but faced with the task
of leopard crawling,
Past Miss Stevenson's cedar-framed wooden fence,
Which I must mention has rusted barbed wire in the grass.
I found that out the hard way,
Wire netted my buttocks like a boneless pork roast.
I received a total of 15 stitches for my recklessness.
I always a sigh with relief when I make it to Mister Ed's place;
An old bed & breakfast lodge turned eerie two-story shack.
Whenever I use his outdoor limescale-plastered faucet to
fill each water jug,
Feels like there are faded eyes watching me from within the
frames
of all eight rooms, above each windowsill.
And that freakish fish weathervane ornamenting his rooftop--
Bobbly-eyed bastard-- gives me the heebie jeebies.
Trust me, if we did not need that water to survive,

I would never trespass at that place.
Mister Ed is one of the nicest men I have ever met;
spends his days caught in a labyrinthine daze.
Woodstock pipe wedged in burnt lips blowing potpourri smoke,
Staring at baggy vanilla snow clouds for something or someone
not there.
We use his hard water to wash our faces and brush our teeth,
Ma can't clean peas or cook mustard greens without water.
I wonder if he has ever seen me from his lonely room.
No one needed to know we could not afford the water bill,
No one needed to know I also stole his sugar cane.
Like the days I sat out of recess at Blue Lake Elementary,
Because I wore mismatched socks to school.
Tried to stay clear of their eyes then too,
With all the times bad luck replayed itself.
Someone had to notice or see something.
My ma does the best she can.
Trying to fit me in with the wealthy kids.
Townsfolk refer to her as "Miss Retha,"
Strong, brawniness withered with age, and a heart of the most
precious metal is my ma,
Who has felt every bit of the Jim Crow reducing blacks
to less than human era.
She chit chat about the days when she raced up to the
local store to buy 10 cent peach soda pops,
Traded the empty bottles and tops back in for half that price.
Being big sister, she helped our widowed grandma around the
house,
By axing and chucking wooden logs into a smokey cast iron
heater.
My uncles also played their parts;
They snapped branching stalks from Native Cabbage Palms
In a red-hot Floridians scorching heat.
Used them to make strong bow & arrows for blue jay hunting.
Poked each of them after a fresh fall,
Strapped their clawed feet together.
Ran home so fast they left skid marks,

In an effort to beat grandma's time-clock.
By the time grandma Elnora left the cottonmouth
& rattlesnake infested fern fields,
They had already stripped, rinsed, seasoned, floured, tossed
the birds in heated oils and eaten them.
Ma, of course, was chef of these feathery gourmets,
She can make anything taste like chicken.
When I asked her why they only hunted blue birds, she said,
"Well, the red birds are a sign that something good is about to
happen."
Every time I've seen a red bird from that day, money followed.
Then came the bill collectors.
Ma's story will always be bigger than some tall tale.
Some blue ox setting a wicked wild river straight has nothing
on her.
A great ma is the one thing I have working in my favor.
As I proceed to peddle to the Can Crush, my friends
wave me on with Papier-mâché hand fans.
My mind can't help but wonder if they deem me a charity case.
It would probably eat me up on the inside, If I cared (I do),
Upon arrival at Can Crush, old man Willis meets and greets
me.
An old, risen-from-the-cracks of poverty-stricken streets, black
man,
Whose government pays less than the minimum wage.
Scaling each and every nasty bag of cans that comes in.
All those years with no pay increase.
Do you know the place where the mind travels
when you no longer give a damn?
If you could travel that odyssey, you would surely find him
there.
Knew from the way he looked at me every visit,
He knew I was padding those cans with dirt to add weight.
I'm assuming he feels it is not his money to lose.
Who can blame the poor man?
Twenty-something odd years at this job,
Getting it from the mud.

No chance in hell of climbing the property ladder,
I'll gladly pocket these wrinkled faces and ride away.
Following each visit to the Can Crush, I would first stop by
Mister Kirkland's to fill my bag with 1 cent candies.
Uncle Pistol only lives a few blocks away from the
Convenient store.
Whenever I go to his place, he'd have more cans for me.
Wasn't much of a drinker, but he kept several soda pop cans.
Considered this a huge blessing,
Never found a roach in one of those.
Uncle Pistol owned an antiquated vinyl
collection, like no other.
His entire home wall to wall to ceiling covered,
with record sleeves.
Some had no more than a scratch,
Some brand spanking new looks.
Visiting him was like walking into a record shop
in the 60s, 70s, and 80s.
His home is the world's biggest vision board.
Diana's "Lady Sing the Blues" is his most spun record.
Elvis, Mayfield, The Rat Pack, The Stylistics, Stevie Wonder,
The Supremes, The Rolling Stones, The Beatles, The Beach
Boys;
The man has them all..
On the lone empty space on the living room wall,
There is an old Henry Rifle hanging up.
Not sure of the significance behind it,
I am sure it has some stories to tell.
When I returned to Red City, the gang were still at it,
Playing "red light, green light, 1-2-3" in the middle of the road.
Darn-near getting run over by every horn-blower passing by.
Before I could say a single word about how much I made,
Betsie opened her lion roaring mouth:

"Boyyy, you so gawt damn stank & filthy!
Not sure if yo mama ever taught you this.
Soap & wauter cures all kinds of funk!"

143

Of all the people who would crack jokes,
Had to be the only girl in my bandmates of misfits.
I was not about to have a jab session with her,
My only comeback before pushing my wheels up the road:
"Keep my momma out of yo mouth.
Please & thank you!"
Now, can't help but think to myself,
I wonder if my family have used all the water jugs.
If not, an unrelaxing cold bath would do me some good.
Only echoes of an aging house when I enter the front door.
To my surprise, someone made enough to pay the
electricity bill.
Going to throw my legs over this recliner's arm,
This being a better time than any to catch a classic
blaxploitation flick.
Maybe I will watch "Foxy Brown," "Three the Hard Way,"
"Blacula," and "The Human Tornado?"
I would follow the cliché by saying, "In that order."
Since the doorknob could turn any second or minute now,
It would be more beneficial to put my fresh thoughts on paper.
Going to spill clammy, inkwell, achromatic colors
Onto sheets of silent majestic paper skin
Perhaps stroking lucid imaginations of a new world,
Of a different me.
Knowing a new pair of sneaks will someday take me far away:
To a place where no telescope is needed to bring stars into
focus;
Where positives sit low, negatives sit high
Aboard life's chameleon skinned teeterboard;
Where there is no such thing as a microwavable beef patty
With 42 different ingredients- None including beef.
Please take me to that necessary place!

This motivates me to write a poem, I will call:

"Grime Doesn't Glitter Like Gold:"
by E.D. Small

Grubby-faced, nails, and hands,
Or perchance a filth-filled life,
May all define this boy
Who has wronged every one of his rights.
Never hand and kneed back and forth,
Trash-landed from the beak of a stork.
No other choice but right-out walk,
No other choice but to right-out talk.
The hammer on this hardhead constantly dropped,
So, my intuition had long been shot.

If my ticker's able to pulsate to a steady beat,
Mulish strength will not allow me to dare get weak.
Forever swamped by my flaws,
Always found myself waist deep.
Grime has an expensive cost,
Its price, far from cheap.
If I don't tread weak,
It could land me underneath.
Probably somewhere around six feet.
Regardless of where I've been,
Or, where I may have to go,
There's one thing that I know,
Nothing could ever muddy my soul.

Grime doesn't glitter like gold,
But whenever I shine,
It will be a sight to behold.

Acknowledgements

A special thanks to God. This would not have been possible with you. Thanks to my Mother & Father, Retha & Donald Small for bringing me into this world. Mother, you will always be my hero mother. I love you always! Thank you to my sister & brother-in-law Donna & Treven Miles. I love you both so much. I appreciate the impact you have had on my life. Bro-in-law, you told me *if you put as much effort into everything, as I do things of little importance, you would be unstoppable.* Thank you for opening my eyes to greatness. There is no looking back after this. Thank you to my beautiful wife Christen for never giving up on me. You are all of the blessings I have ever asked for, all bundled up into one package. I pray we see great success and can sail to paradise to get away from the kids (lol). I love you Lyndon, Sierra & Reyna! Thank you to uncle Arthur & aunt Rose. You have done so much for the family throughout the years, we could never repay you in this lifetime. Thank you to my sisters Love & Keisha Small! I love you both! There is not a thing I would not do for you two. Thank you, Cornelius Fuller, for gifting me with so many golden nuggets during our jogging conversations. Thank you, Ms. Maxine Fuller, Myrna Loy and Ms. Eurma Tisdale, for being the sweet-hearted women you are!

Thank you to my cousins Montrale & Lacey Hamilton, Brian Ward, Lee & Lametriss Wiley, Johnny, Cab, Tee, Shinell & Amaria Birch, Madeline & Qua'Neisha Brockington, Christy Brockington, Brian Ward, Nikeisha & Kentrell Pinkney, Gus Ward, Sharvin Ward, Barbara Ward, Marcus & Michael Brockington, Corey Taylor, Sirrom Senoj, Chris Jones, Larry "Snag" Brockington, Tracy Ward, Muff, Helene, Essie, Drummond Hamilton, Mike Mike, Vern Vern. We are blood We are family.

Let's continue to strive and grow stronger as one. Imagine how beautiful life will be if we can all branch like the tree of life.

To my nephews & nieces: Tadrian Ward, Travanda Miles, Eric Williams, Kendall Miles, Quentin Wyche, Javonshanay Ward, Tomas Ward, Edgar & Crystal Ward, Kenny Lawrence & Princess Bailbonds, JaQuez, Jalayah, Traniyah, Kj, Aj, Shy'na, Peanut, British I love you all! If the world is yours but only if you want it. Go get it! To all of my kinfolks in St. Petersburg, Florida: Aunt Martha, aunt Colleen, Nathaniel, Keisha, Faye, Camille, Felipe, Geneva, Veronica, Howard, Chanika, Lori, Twanna. I love every one of you all.

To my extended family: Karol, Lori, DJ, Kelli, Tenise Jenkins, Amy De Jesus, Sam B, Immanuel & Jena, Pamela, Kim, Andrew Surgick, Kevin Sr. & Shari, Kevin & Shasharaa, Sonny & Robin, & the rest of the Baum & Blackshear family. I love you all!

Friends: Natalie Jackson *(based Civil Trial Lawyer for Trayvon Martin family)*, Jacqueline Weah, Latayvia Stanley, Anthony Judson, Adam McLane, Damion & Jennifer Dunn, Clarence Goosby Jr, Blaze Daniels, Lorenzo "Avoy" Bee, Author Nick Sampson, Author Michael Major, Author Tonia Quarterman, Jamall & Jamira Williams, Tony Smith, Aaron Thompson, Dee Bletcher, Damien Woulard, Lulu, Eddie & Elizabeth Senez, Denise Wright, Dre'chelle Smith, QuePaso Parker, April Barkley, Ced & Telecia Jones, Melva Mims, Tavarious Cooper, Lance Petro, Marchelle Antoinette, LTazzie Taz, Kimberly & Marlana June, John LaCorte, Val Avery, Ruth Davenport, Mike & Rod Jackson, Melissa Martinez, Georgann Mavros-Carnicella, Herman Baptiste, She'nitah & Catoya Johnson, Anna Kopec, Coach Dawson, Davon Jones, Maria Carmen,

Adonna Thurman, Shanika Patterson, Shay Sanders, Ms. Aida Paiva, Elaine Harris, Rasheedah Payne, Maxine Butler, Tamara Birch, Tierney Simmons, Eric West, Rod Thomas, Roy Williams, Willie "Lil Man" Goosby, Raynesha & Bella Bella Goosby, Kyrenia Duggar, Shannon Palmer, Shay Cusack, T-Nicole, King Augo, Tina Desaussure, Monte Patrice, Sherita Staples, Darryl Taylor & Jo Gunn, David Austin, Keturah Jay, Lawrence Campbell, Rachel Moses, Solliett CR, Del Villar, Sherman Edwards, Leslie Ann Donaldson, Kenneth Miles, Janelle Harris, Ms. Cheryl Corey, Krista Franks, Jean Pauline, Jo Hamilton, Dale Smith, Shirley Parks, Mia, Virma Linares, Ben "Superman" Sutphin, Kathy Weaver, Lizamarie Williams, Veronica Woulard, Amanda Thompson, Chris Jackson, Travis & Andrea McKinney, RJ & Sundria Simpson, DD & & Chayla Padgett, Nick Nick Wallery, Cory Mckinney, Marissa Blanchard, Debo & Shameka Grant Edwards, Skeeter West, Calvin Wells, Tamara Layne, Diyonna Dukes, Lloyd Mccray, Martavious Carter, James Hampton, Marissa Blanchard, Coach Taz, Aisha Harris, Disa Smith, David Austin, Julie Hickox, Yolanda Graham, Brandy Stephens, Brandy Green, Jay & Debbie Fisher, Freddy James Fisher, Mike Davis, Kiheenia, Dimary, Luis Santaliz, Julia Kennick, Julie Ryan Murray, Aaron Asuncion, Christina Zebelle, Cassandra Jones Ward, Fred Williams, Marco Solomon, Xavier Coleman, JoAnna Cook Ratliff, Diana Salas, Frederick Evans, Sameme Ferguson, Nick Eldridge, Lucius Brooks, Mia Howard, Tionna, Denise Wood-Evans, Mike Davis, Krista Franks,Tony Johnson, Marquis Heflin, Crystal Lewis, Sandra Blessed, Leticia Clark Nweze, Lemele Scott, Virma Linares, Monte Patrice, Latanya Webb, Kayonni Keith, Jennifer Tarntino, Jody Ayers, Anquernette Bennett, Awula Mida, Don & Cathy Sutphin, Elaine Lyons, Jason Keirsey, Denise Tucker, Tara Tara, Tasha Azama, Laceil Jones, Jessica Miller and Lee Miller, Rhea Robinson, Shayla Walker, Sosee Thomas, Prince Phillip & Louise Breland, Alissa Lapinski, Shalawn Langston, Tyron Booker, CC Hayden, Nicole Jackson Thomas, John Dill &

Sandy Mullendill, Tracey Shivers, Stacey Shropshire, Albert Miles, Gee King, Sylvester Frett, Austell, Denise Tucker, Jason Keirsey, Tony "the Tiger" Romero, Raymond Huffman, Tanesha Cooper, Aisha Harris, Jalisa Evans, Mimi Williams, Fred Mccaskill, Natasha Howard, Robert Nutt, Luis Acosta, Michele Ward, Robert Earl Jr, Donny Cormier, Okoye Black Panther, Asha Lane, Billy Jackson, Fiona A. Brown-Guyton, Liza Avila, KC & Antwan Brown, Coleman Butler, Steve Graham, Katy & Manny Baptiste, Donald & Persephone Woulard, Kera Redman, Michele Brown, Elysia Napoli, Ashley Lennon, Chesney Johnson, J. Gray (IG:thejgrey), Christopher Reighn, Danisha Chisolm, Shawn Medvar, Shawn Colbert, Telecia Coleman Williams, Betty Smith, Terresa Williams, Andrew Paez, Beth Eaton, Dee Carpenter, Francisco Ortiz, Anita Farrington

Businesses: Teacher Markesha James & the students of Thompson Street Tabernacle of Praise, New St. John Missionary Baptist Church (Lead Pastor Bishop Eugene R. Collier III & First Lady Kimberly Collier, Mother Hazel Collier-May, Reverand Barbara Powell & the rest of the church family), Deland Neighborhood Center, Dee Carpenter, All of my Stetson University family, Deland Bulldogs School & Football Organization, Simpson Marketing Services, Accident and Injury Chiropractic in Deltona (Florida), Daytona Beach News-Journal, H.O.O.D. News Global (Help Others Out Despairing), Goozay Jahbar: Hair Growth and Beard Spray for Men, The Leach Firm, Margaret Made Wingz, The West Volusia Beacon, St Barnabes Episcopal Church (Deland), Salvation Army (Deland), Deland Chisolm Center, Stetson Baptist Church (Deland)

In memory of: My grandmother Elnora Brockington. Who I wish could be here to see her grandson become the first author in the family. I love her now & forevermore. My uncle Freddy who passed away on Thanksgiving Day 2020. Will miss talking to him about his losing Cowboys & my losing Jaguars, I will love him always! My brothers Kendall Ward & Victor Small. I wish they could be here to see this. We would have a celebra tion out of this world. I will always love my brothers, who left far too early. At the hand of gun violence. My sister Charletha Ward. I love her with all of the affection I can muster. She was had a heart of gold. If I could trade lives with anyone, she would be here today. I miss you sister.

A special thanks goes out to an amazing team:
Bianca Bowers, Brittany Baum, & Natalie Duffy.

Words cannot describe how awesome you ladies are. There is no way this project could have been brought into existence without your hard work & commitment. It is never an easy task to interpret someone else's vision. I pray we can all gather success from this project and do it all over again.

www.ingramcontent.com/pod-product-compliance
Lightning Source LLC
Chambersburg PA
CBHW031551040426
42452CB00006B/263